The Overgate

Douglas Phillips and Ron Thompson

INTRODUCTION

When older Dundonians are reminiscing on the Overgate of long ago their eyes take on a dreamy-like expression as if recalling carefree days at the seaside or childhood picnics in idyllic settings. The reality couldn't be in greater contrast. The original Overgate was latterly 16 acres of crumbling tenements and congested backlands, of slum housing and tumbledown shops, of poverty and much else besides. Children were warned not to go there unescorted. It was an area which blighted the centre of Dundee and had a notoriety known in other parts of Scotland. But despite this flawed reputation the Overgate, with its proud and friendly dwellers and irrepressible characters, exerted a great drawing power on others. To walk its narrow, twisting, cobbled thoroughfare was to experience a homeliness born of hardship. It was a vibrant, couthie township within the heart of a city and it is much missed.

During its long history the Overgate produced and harboured people of varying social backgrounds. Anna, Duchess of Buccleuch and Monmouth, was born there in 1651. So, earlier, was Hector Boece, the famous 16th century Scots historian. Several hundred years later, in 1938, the boxing skill of Freddie Tennant brought the Scottish Flyweight professional title back to his humble abode in the Overgate. In the troubled times between both world wars Mary Brooksbank, poet and tribune, who had also lived there, fought famously for the rights of the under-privileged. During the previous century Fanny Wright had campaigned similarly in America, after a childhood partly spent in close proximity to the deprivation of the Overgate. Here, also, famous military battles were waged long ago – and it was in the Overgate that the Scottish Mint was at one time located before the Union. Yes, the Overgate was without doubt the most famous part of Dundee and the most central of all its precincts. But all this was swept away in the late 1950's and 60's when bulldozers reduced the entire precinct to rubble and dust.

Originally Doug Phillips and I had no intention of resurrecting the place in words and drawings. Having recently completed a trilogy on old Dundee we had decided to close down our department of nostalgia and rest in peace. But when local folk kept harping on about the Overgate of old, a ghost which refuses to go away, we decided to have another dip into the past and put some flesh on fact and memory. This is what we have come up with.

Ron Thompson
April, 1996

DOUG PHILLIPS is held in high esteem as an artist, his oils and watercolours being regularly exhibited at prestige galleries throughout Scotland, including the Royal Scottish Academy. Several of his paintings have become popular limited edition prints. His drawings of Dundee past and present are equally in demand and inflict much nostalgia on Dundonians now settled abroad. It is this particular skill he now deploys in these pages. His work has featured on the front cover of Readers Digest and his illustrations have enhanced over a hundred children's books in Britain and the U.S.A. Doug is a native Dundonian.

RON THOMPSON is now a freelance writer and broadcaster, having been a reporter for over 45 years. Trained on the newspapers of D. C. Thomson, for whom he now pens a weekly column in the Dundee Courier, he later worked on several "nationals," including the Daily Herald and Sunday Express, before spending 26 years in front of camera for Grampian Television. His books include "Never a Dull Moment," an account of his early years in television, and "Beyond 2001," the story of a Dundee engineer who believed he had invented a flying saucer. Ron, who was awarded the M.B.E. in 1991, also has his roots in Dundee.

PREFACE

When the Overgate first appeared as Argyllgait on the map of Dundee about 800 years ago it consisted of little more than a cluster of single and double-storey wooden houses. These were said to have been occupied by Gaelic-speaking tradesmen and their families who had moved down from the Highlands. If this were so it could account for the original name of Argyllgait. Others, however, claim it was named after a noble family of Argyll who resided in the street. In any event the change to Overgate was made during the 16th century by which time Flukergait had been renamed Nethergate, "nether", of course, meaning "lower". With the street above – Argyllgait – being on the upper side of Nethergate it then became known as Overgate. By this time it was one of Dundee's main arteries to the west, stretching beyond the City Churches and now one of the most fashionable places in which to live. It consisted of many fine, stone-built town mansions, with gardens and orchards to the rear, and good quality tenements – a high-class residential thoroughfare occupied by wealthy merchants and members of the local aristocracy. However, by the turn of the 17th century these burgesses and titled gentry began moving out to grand houses being built on the outskirts of the town, with the accommodation they left behind being gradually taken over by working-class folk – many of them spinners and weavers – who also set up inferior dwellings and workshops in the backlands. From that point the Overgate was never going to be the same again. It was heading down the social ladder. By the mid-17th century the Overgate had possibly stretched, in a crooked line, almost to its ultimate length of 500 yards, ending at what was later to become West Port and Tay Street. The backlands had continued to fill up with assorted buildings – a process called repletion – although even in the 18th century there was still some open ground in the Overgate surrounded by hedges.

By the 19th century, however, it was a heavily congested area, a warren of closes and vennels, pends and alleys, as Dundee's population soared dramatically with the expansion of the textile industry, a development which resulted in the appearance of many three and four-storey sub-standard tenements in a programme of industrial house building throughout Dundee. At this stage the Overgate, with many of its older buildings having been replaced over the years, was intersected along its entire length by a herring-bone pattern of other thoroughfares, including Tally Street, Thorter Row, Barrack Street, Lindsay Street, Long Wynd, and Tay Street. By the turn of the present 20th century it had become notorious for its bad housing and general unsightly appearance, an ugly blot on the city landscape with a density of 400 persons per acre compared to an average of 36 for the whole city. In 1910 the city engineer and architect, James Thomson, a man of great vision, submitted a plan to the Town Council for central improvements which included the widening and modernising of the Overgate. He envisaged clearing the buildings from the foot of the Overgate on the south side right up to Tally Street and converting that island area – bounded also by the High Street – into public gardens dominated by statues and a fountain. In 1913 the Corporation was set to proceed but the scheme was shelved the following year on the outbreak of the First World War.

Another twenty-three years were to pass before the Overgate redevelopment again became an urgent issue. This time the Corporation engaged Dr Thomas Adams, a London town planning consultant, to draw up plans. These were to turn the Overgate into a boulevard-type thoroughfare ending with a roundabout at its western end from which would radiate a pattern of five roads. As with the Thomson plan, he envisaged the bottom area of the Overgate up to Tally Street being permanently cleared of buildings, but with the reclaimed space being added to the High Street to ease the circulation of vehicular traffic. This scheme was also approved by the Corporation towards the end of 1937, but once again the outbreak of war – this time in 1939 – put a new Overgate into cold storage. It wasn't until 1950 that the city fathers took another hard look at the future of the area by engaging the services of W. Dobson Chapman and Partners who designed a totally new precinct to meet the needs of a post-war urban community. This scheme was based on a modern shopping centre stretching right up to Long Wynd, free from traffic and with all commercial premises being serviced from the rear – and that was basically the plan finally adopted by the Corporation and approved by the Secretary of State for Scotland in August 1960. This provided a two-deck shopping mall with over a hundred retail units linked by stairs and ramps and included department stores, office blocks and a hotel.

And so in 1961 – this time, thankfully, undeterred by war – a start was made at last to rebuild the new Overgate. It was the first town centre redevelopment scheme in Scotland and it was officially opened by Princess Margaret in April, 1970. The new precinct had cost over £4 million and from the date of the first Thomson plan had taken 60 years to accomplish. In a striking example of "clean sweep" planning the old Overgate of small shops and teeming tenements had completely disappeared – apart, of course, from the City Churches and St. Mary's Tower – to be replaced with a purpose-built centre devoid of housing and constructed in a building style described as concrete cubism. Despite all the undoubted advantages this had over what was there before in terms of functionalism, the new Overgate has never generated the same

affection as the old. Before the redevelopment got under way the city's Lord Provost, the late Dr Maurice McManus, said: "I look forward very keenly to the day when we can, once again, regard with pride this ancient and honourable thoroughfare." Many would say that day has still to come.

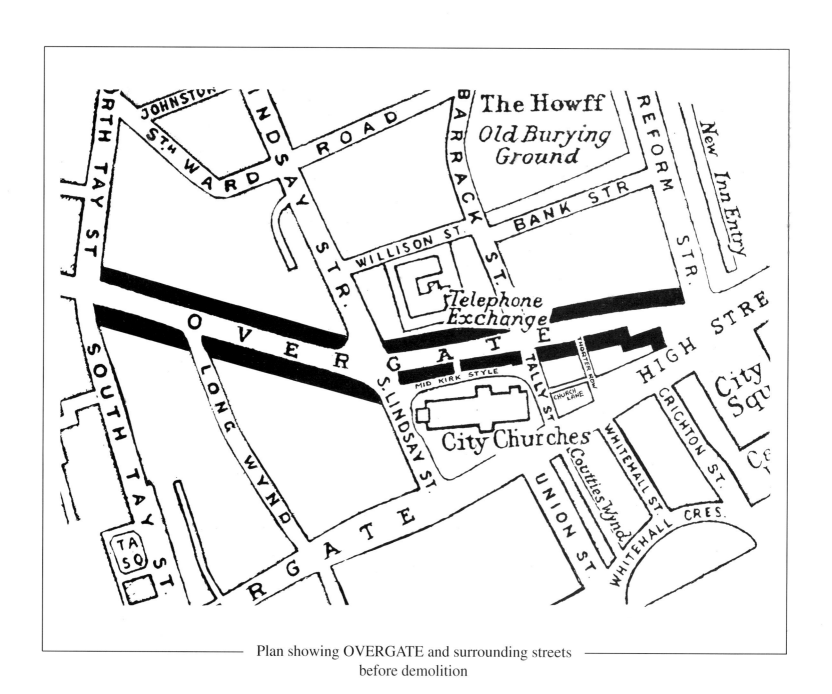

Plan showing OVERGATE and surrounding streets
before demolition

The Overgate

As still remembered

SETTING THE SCENE

The old Overgate was in a world of its own, a crazy jigsaw of small shops and dilapidated houses in dingy, over-crowded tenements, laced together by a pattern of narrow streets and cluttered backlands. It was a planner's nightmare, Dundee's most notorious slum, designated by many as a den of iniquity but seen by others as having a heart of gold, a rumbustious welcome forever on its mat for the jostling crowds that surged along its twisting length. It wasn't called the Nile for nothing. There was certainly no place like it on a Saturday night, particularly in the earlier part of this century when the entire precinct became one big, open-air theatre with a cast of thousands and a bill of fare to satisfy every appetite. To cash in on pay day many of the shops stayed open until ten or eleven and the streets were lined with hawkers' stalls, their wares illuminated by the flare of naphtha lamps. Pubs did a roaring trade and as drunken brawls erupted on the pavements religious groups sermonised on the evils of drink and attempted to convert the unconvertible. There was also a great carnival atmosphere in the Overgate with a wide selection of side shows for those willing to spend a penny or two. Captain Texas, for example, was a deadly marksman, 6 feet tall with a drooping moustache and dressed like a cowboy. Lying on his back on top of a wicker basket with a .22 Winchester rifle, he would shatter a sugar cube balanced on a cork which, in turn, was perched on the head of his young daughter, little Dodo Texas. Mexican Pedro Gonzales also diced with death – this time as a knife thrower using his Red Indian squaw as a colourful target. Across the road, in a shop at the corner of Long Wynd, there was a flea circus where the performers, in a large museum case, were attached by fine silken threads to imitation gun carriages and coaches. The circus master, using a long, thin, steel rod, gently prodded the insects until the vehicles jerked into motion. A doorman assured everyone that the fleas had been born and bred in the Overgate. There was also Captain Wallace, the fire-eater, operating out of a former toy shop. Every hour he would dip his sword into a compound of flaming sawdust and paraffin and make the lot disappear down his throat, telling his audience later that this was excellent medicine for nagging wives. Another of the Overgate entrepreneurs had taken over other premises to exhibit a giant shark landed by a Dundee trawler at Carolina Port. Unfortunately, this coincided with a heatwave and, despite giving the shark several coats of whitewash, the stench became so unbearable the prize catch was removed by order of the sanitary authorities – and that was saying something in the Overgate. There were many other fairground attractions too: bearded ladies, two-headed dogs, wild men from Borneo, dancing cannibals, the biggest rat in the world, and the headless woman.

Street musicians were also ten a penny. They ranged from pipers and "moothie" players to fiddlers, accordionists, and tin whistlers. There was also a kerbside singer called White Willie, on account of his near-white hair, whose raucous voice could render only one number, "When the Roses Come Again." Add to all this the buster stalls, the tripe shops, and the "chippers," together with a great mass of humanity which included Irish navvies, Indian sailors off the jute boats, and English soldiers encamped at nearby Buddon, and you had all the ingredients of a place in the grip of a Saturday night fever. Indeed, these were the days when anyone in Dundee seeking to describe a scene approaching bedlam would simply resort to the well-known phrase – "It was just like the Overgate on a Saturday night."

COUNTRY FOLK

The Overgate was a powerful magnate for the country folk on market days, Saturdays, and at feeing times. On these latter occasions farmers would hire their hands for the term ahead, with both parties then spitting on their palms and sealing the contract with a hearty handshake. This is not exactly how political leaders fix policy these days at world summits but it worked then in farming circles. And with business concluded the farmer and farm servant, attired in rough suits, bonnets, and tackety boots, took to the Overgate to meet up with families and friends for a day out in their favourite part of Dundee. For a spot of lunch they would invariably head for Franchi's, the Overgate's top eating place where the spacious restaurant on the upper floor looked out over the main thoroughfare. Here, before the last war, a three-course lunch cost 1s 6d with a menu offering five soups, three types of fish, fifteen meat dishes, and a dozen puddings. Having taken their fill, the next stop might be a few doors up to Peter Fagan's, outfitters and licensed broker, where a three-piece suit could be had for a pound, a good pair of "cords" for 12s 6d, and a bunnet for a bob. Then it was on to the Poets' Box at No. 207, a dingy, gas-lit shop, jam-packed with sheet music and songs of all descriptions – from Scots and local folk numbers to songs that celebrated the Masonic and temperance movements. There was also a wide range of recitations, parodies, extracts of popular readings, and stump speeches. According to the catalogue there were "millions to choose from." The Box was run by Lowden Macartney, who had worked for many years on a New York newspaper. Installing a hand-operated printing press in his back shop, he churned out thousands of sheets which he sold at a few coppers each. Farm workers, with their bothy entertainment, were among his best customers and it was not unusual to find a ploughman in the shop, his "doolichter" bonnet pushed back, bawling out a ballad as a guide to the music he was after. For Dundee folk local songs were particularly popular with such numbers as Along the Magdalen Green, Cadgers o' Dundee, Down by the Yeaman Shore, Fall of the Tay Bridge, Dundee Nell, and Come and See the Whale. But sheets of prose were also greatly in demand in days when many couldn't read and were willing to pay a penny to attend public readings in a local hall. Macartney's catalogue therefore offered many pieces suitable for these occasions, extracts from Shakespeare, Longfellow, and Walter Scott, mixed in with less classical items such as The Bapteesement o' the Bairn, The Battle of Pea Soup, and The Virtues of Holloway's Ointment. And the evening could end on a cautionary note for the country folk with the final verse of At the Back o' Reres Hill:

So all you country lasses, a warnin' tak by me ,
And be sure and choose your company when ye
    gang intae Dundee;
And beware o' bachelor laddies doon by yon
    Baxter's Mill,
For they're sure tae gar ye lose yer way at the
    back o' Reres Hill.

On this note it is perhaps appropriate to mention that Dundee's first vending machine for condoms, installed before the last war, was on the wall just outside the Poets' Box.

BUSTERS

Eating places in the Overgate – apart from Franchi's – tended to be of the humble variety. They included chip shops, tripe shops, and "cookies," all offering basic fare at keen prices, either sitting in or taking out. But possibly the most famous of all was the "buster" stall at the Saturday market in Mid Kirk Style, which ran between the main spine of the Overgate and the rear of the City Churches. Busters represented a unique dish which consisted of peas and chips served with a savoury bree and lots of vinegar. A plateful was a real tightener, often making you feel you might burst – hence the term "buster." Had this concoction been given a more fashionable name busters might even have finished up on classy menus. As it was this offering remained in the realm of grass-roots cuisine, served up in the most humble surroundings. The buster stall was nothing more than a big wooden shed with a canvas roof and long forms for seating round the walls. The cooking was done in black pots on a big, fiercely-hot coke brazier in the middle of the stall in full view of the diners who, on a winter's night, drew added comfort from the heat of the open-plan kitchen. At other times, however, the brazier created sauna-like conditions, as remembered by Doug Smithers to this day. "It was like being in a furnace room," he says. "We kept having to turn round on the form like a roast on a spit to escape the searing heat." Busters were introduced to Dundee by the de Gernier family, originally of Brussels in Belgium. One of the sons, Edward, married a French girl and through the friendship of a Scotsman arrived in Blairgowrie to work in the local jute mills. In 1874 the couple settled in Dundee and took a stall in the Greenmarket (later to become Shore Terrace) serving chipped potatoes, peas, and vinegar from a small tent. This novel combination met with instant success. Indeed, Edward de Gernier, a shoemaker to trade,

claimed he was the first person to introduce chips into Britain. Later the buster stall moved to the Overgate and when eventually displaced from there under the demolition programme finally went indoors for a spell in Hawkhill. But the "camping" spirit of the original buster stall was never recaptured in a permanent building and in the early 1960's busters became a taste of the past. No longer do we hear the cry ringing out from the rickety wooden shed – "Big peas and lang tatties," a unique marketing slogan if ever there was one. But the de Gerniers live on in Dundee. George de Gernier, great-great-grandson of buster fame, is a well-known public figure, serving on Dundee City Council. "Being taken by my father down to the family buster stall in the Overgate is one of the outstanding memories of my childhood," says George. "There always seemed to be a happy, carefree atmosphere in the place."

Then eh'd toddle doon the Overgate,

For a buster if you please;

Eh mind the smell and eh mind the taste,

O' the chips and the mushy green peas;

The wumman that served them wiz awfae fine,

She dipped the plate in a bucket o' watter;

Then wiped the spane on her peenie – syne,

Before pourin' vinegar a' ower yer platter.

POLICE

Being a policeman on the Overgate beat gave you a unique insight into the way the other half lived. George McLaren, who served thirty years on the local force before retiring as a sergeant in 1968, received an "education" second to none. He is to this day, however, adamant that the Overgate, although no paragon of virtue, was never a hotbed of crime and what anti-social behaviour there was could be largely attributed to its floating population. Nevertheless, George, in his day, had to sort out a bewildering number of problems which afflicted his charges in the Overgate patch. Many of them were of a purely domestic nature. One winter's night during the last war a knock on the police box door in Thorter Row revealed a shivering wee woman with one eye, dressed only in a faded white nightie. George was just finishing off his "piece" at the time. "Meh man has pit me oot," wailed the wifie, tears streaming down a face old before its time. "Will ye come up and gie him a fleg?" George duly made his way to the single end and remonstrated with the erring husband who, inevitably, had been drinking. P.C. No. 122 duly warned him that such conduct was not to be tolerated, before seeing the evicted wife safely back in bed with her penitent husband then putting off the gas and closing the door behind him. Case ended. This was standard police procedure at the time. Giving anti-social tenants and their off-spring a "fleg" – the Scots expression for a fright – usually brought results. Nowadays such incidents would possibly involve social workers, marriage guidance counsellors, Samaritans, human rights groups, and perhaps even an appointment with a clinical psychologist. But when George was a Bobby on the Overgate beat giving people a fleg was often good enough.

MURDER

At one time, when murders were less frequent than they are now, a violent death would create banner headlines and rock a whole city on its heels. The Overgate provided such a drama towards the end of its own life in September, 1956, when the body of a young, attractive mother was found in an attic house at 15 Mid Kirk Style, late one Saturday night. She had been strangled with a tablecloth. The tenement had been mostly evacuated to await demolition under the redevelopment programme. The dead woman was Mrs Jean Lloyd, the 24 year-old mother of two children, who had lived on the Douglas council estate at the other end of the city. Her husband was serving a prison sentence at the time of the tragedy. Police activity at the scene attracted groups of sightseers and it was soon established that Mrs Lloyd had been shopping in the Overgate earlier on the Saturday and had bought chocolates in a cafe where she was well-known to the assistants. Someone said they had seen her going into the tenement close with a man, who reappeared shortly after. Jean, a former pupil of Harris Academy, who had worked for a grocer in the High Street and in the kiosk at the Gaumont Cinema, was well-known as a pianist. Large crowds turned out for her funeral, first outside her home in Balunie Avenue and then at Balgay Cemetery where the service was conducted by the Rev. Phillip Lee, chaplain to the city's Welfare Services Department. A 36 year-old farm labourer from Newbigging, Angus, had earlier appeared in court charged with the murder and was remanded in Perth Prison. Two months later it was decided no criminal proceedings would be taken against him and he was set free.

HOUSING

The Overgate had some of the worst housing in Dundee and much of the area had degenerated into a slum by the time it was eventually flattened for redevelopment. Before the last war the Salvation Army had its slum headquarters at No. 219 Overgate and from 1903 lady health visitors, venturing together into slum quarters of the city like the Overgate, had their lives insured by the Town Council for £150 each. A typical report would refer to the kitchen of a city house as being clean and tidy but with the room next door "often covered in cobwebs and spittum, giving an offensive odour … frequently there were two or three pails of filth standing in the room." The health visitors often found old women looking after three or four infants and it was a daily occurrence to find half-a-dozen unattended children hiding under the bed, having mistaken the visitors as school board officers. Such were the consequences of mothers forced

out to work. Outside lavatories shared by many families was the norm. Bathrooms in the Overgate were almost a curiosity. Many of the tenements had a large hall or lobby on every floor – each with a large communal iron sink – with corridors leading off to a cluster of flats. Rats were not uncommon. In today's language the Overgate was an area of multiple deprivation with low rents attracting the poorest families. But many of its inhabitants were proud of their homes, some of them quite spacious and beautifully kept. One old woman in a single end stacked all her old newspapers five feet high in the room, leaving only a narrow passage to the bed, sink, and fireside. The weight of the paper must have strained the floor joints to breaking point. But although the Overgate tenements were dilapidated by the end, many of them had lasted for centuries and were a tribute to the building standards of their time.

MODEL LODGING HOUSES

Model lodging houses, used mainly by people of no fixed abode, were once a feature of life in Dundee. Between the two wars the Overgate had five of these communal sleeping places, giving a total of 238 beds for men and women, and were regularly inspected by the local authority for cleanliness and general administration. Several shops in the Overgate would sell the residents a poke of milk, a masking of tea, and a slice of bread and butter for a few coppers. Sleeping in these dormitories could be a dodgy business when it came to protecting one's property. Which is why most people slept with their clothes under the mattress or pillow and with the legs of the bed firmly planted inside their boots. As a young policeman serving in the Overgate in the late 1950's, James Brooks vividly remembers the night he was called to a lodging house to assist an ambulanceman in stretchering out one of the residents who was suffering an asthmatic attack. He recalls: "On entering the room the entire floor space was taken up with beds all occupied by males in deep slumber. The patient was in the far corner and, as there was virtually no space between the beds, we were forced to walk over them to remove the poor man. To compound matters he could not lie down due to his breathlessness and had to sit upright on the stretcher in order to breathe. The return journey over the beds was a nightmare trying to retain one's balance on the ever-moving surface, aggravated by the indelicate balance of the patient and the verbal onslaught of the other residents who had been rudely awakened from their drunken slumber. After a few coups, fortunately on soft mattresses, our man was safety ensconced in the ambulance and transported to hospital." Model lodging houses are now a thing of the past.

FREDDIE TENNANT

There was much street fighting in the Overgate, usually between those who had been ejected from the pubs, and the police were constantly carting off the combatants to Bell Street. In fact, some people would wander up the Overgate on a Saturday night just to spectate at these open-air contests. But it was the Overgate which produced one of Dundee's best-loved professional fighters, Freddie Tennant, a real local hero who brought the Scottish Flyweight title back to the city in 1938 and once defeated the immortal Benny Lynch. Freddie was born in the Fife mining village of Lochgelly in 1913, one of a large family who moved to Dundee the following year and settled in the Overgate. He took up boxing after leaving Tay Street School and, with little money coming into the house, went off to fight in the fairground booths, first at the local Riverside and Gussie Parks where he would often go six rounds for five bob. Later he worked the booths all over England at a weekly wage which ranged from fifteen shillings to two pounds, sometimes fighting six times in two days and earning himself the reputation of being a determined and entertaining scrapper. He fought professionally for nearly twenty years, with a top purse of £90, and shared the ring five times with Benny Lynch, the eventual world champion, loosing three times, drawing once, but beating him on points on a memorable night in Glasgow in 1932. Freddie bowed out in the Caird Hall in 1946 (shades of the booths!) but wasn't finally counted out until the age of 74 in 1987. Unlike Dick McTaggart, the Dundee golden boy of world boxing, Freddie didn't merit a place in Madame Tussaud's Waxworks. But the memory of a doughty fighter lives on.

MARY BROOKSBANK

Mary Brooksbank was another bonny fechter to come out of the Overgate, although she inflicted her blows upon opponents with powerful oratory rather than with flailing fists. Between the wars she was a leading campaigner for the under-privileged and the unemployed. Later the pen became her weapon as she resorted to poem and song to express her anger at the deprivation she had suffered and witnessed throughout her life. Born in Aberdeen, her parents moved to the foot of the Overgate in 1905. Mary was in the mills before she was fourteen, shifting bobbins twelve hours a day for a pittance, an experience which inspired her famous jute mill song "Oh, Dear Me":

> Oh, dear me, the mill's gaen fest,
> The puir wee shifters canna get a rest,
> Shiftin' bobbins, coorse and fine,
> They fairly mak' ye work for your ten and nine.

With the country in ferment over social unrest, Mary joined the Communist Party in the early 1920's and took an active part in local demonstrations, being jailed several times as a revolutionary. On one occasion, while being examined by the prison doctor, she was asked such questions as the date of the Battle of Waterloo. "I got the feeling," she said later, "that they were questioning my sanity, not being able to understand why I was campaigning for basic rights." She herself could never understand how men could be so brave in war and yet submit to the social crimes of capitalism. Mary was also a fine singer and was known to have sung in the streets of Tayport when her husband was ill and unemployed. She died a widow in 1978 at the age of 80 after publishing her book of poems, "Sidlaw Breezes."

PUBS

Dundee has always had its fair share of pubs and within the city the Overgate was always an important drinking sector. Indeed, the entrance to the old Overgate was for many years heralded by a huge illuminated sign on the roof of General Monck's headquarters which, in coloured lights, spelled out "Yellow Label Whisky." There were about thirteen pubs lining the main street alone, their names reeling off the tongue like famous regiments: The Pump, Unity Tavern, Parliamentary Bar, The Swan, J. B. Lawson's, Old Steeple Bar, Anchor Tavern, The Star, Harp and Thistle, A1 Bar, Yeaman's Bar, New Bank Bar, and the Variety Bar. Many others were to be found in the immediate vicinity: Anderson's Tavern, Perthshire Tavern, New Imperial Hotel, Red Lion, Mercat Cross, Zanzibar, and Dundee Arms Tavern. There was also the famous Cafe Royal in Thorter Row with its impressive Victorian interior, a favourite howff for sporting and theatrical celebrities along with jute wallahs home on leave from Calcutta and reporters and photographers from neighbouring newspaper offices. From midday every Saturday these pubs thronged with customers and in the early days those who finished up outside the worse of wear were carted off by the police in the drunks' barrow. Despite the protestations of Dundee's prohibitionist MP Neddy Scrymgeour, and many local temperance groups, the Overgate was always a lucrative place for the licensed trade.

Oh, as Eh went doon the Overgate,

Eh met wee Johnny Scobie,

He says tae me 'Dae ye tak a half'?

Says Eh 'Man, that's meh hoabby'!

CAFES

The Overgate was well endowed with cafes and other establishments which served food and non-alcoholic refreshments and the Venice was one such popular rendezvous at the bottom end, near the High Street. It boasted a soda fountain, a miniature one-arm bandit on the counter downstairs, and an early form of juke box music which proved a big hit with customers before the last war. Jim Donald, long-time resident in New Jersey, U.S.A., has fond memories of the big pianola which stood between the two upstairs tearooms. "There was a small, model piano on the wall in each of the tearooms and by putting a penny into either of them you got a tune on the pianola," he remembers. "It was the nearest thing the Overgate had to a nightclub." Round the corner in Church Lane was the unpretentious Penguin Cafe, well-known for its choice of filled rolls. But there was no place quite like Greenhill's the chemist, half-way up on the right, where, as in American drug stores, a refreshment service was offered to customers over and above the medicines dispensed on the premises. This consisted of a range of coloured concoctions of various flavours, all fizzed up with spoonfuls of white powder. The speciality of the house, however, was Sarsparilla, better known as a "Sass", which was the colour and taste of liquorice – a black draft claimed by many to have the properties of a laxative and the cure for a hang-over.

Sugarelly water, black as the lum,

Gather up your preens and ye'll a' get some.

CHIP SHOPS

For many years before and after the last war the Zanre family ran a couple of chip shops in the Overgate. Giulia (pronounced Julia) manned the frier at the White Rose at the corner of South Lindsay Street while brother Joe looked after the Grand further up at No. 171. Both regarded these times as among the best of their lives. The chips for both shops were prepared in the kitchen at the Grand, with those for the White Rose being barrowed down the street in special containers ready for frying. They opened at four, to get ready for the mill workers coming in on their way home covered with stour, and closed at midnight. Joe remembers American tourists promenading the Overgate before the war and entering his shop full of amazement. "We have nothing like this in the States," they told him. "We just come here for the fish suppers." The White Rose, with its high-backed booths in the sitting-room, was a favourite meeting place for courting couples, particularly during the war with Dundee's influx of Polish soldiers and French and Dutch sailors. These "black out" years also brought a shortage of fish and wrapping paper. Very often they would only fry haddock twice a night and some customers would turn up with their own plates for a carry-out. The White Rose also had an ice-cream parlour which excelled in iced drinks. "Sometimes people would come in early on a Sunday morning and plead for an iced drink because they were 'in the horrors'" (suffering from a hangover), explained Giulia. "But because of some strange by-law we weren't allowed to sell these drinks on the Sabbath if they were to be consumed on the premises before 11 a.m., even although they were non-alcoholic. However, if the customer lived nearby I simply delivered the order to their home." This was all part of the service of a typical Overgate shopkeeper.

COFFEE STALLS

Coffee stalls were another source of refreshment in the Overgate area, not exactly the haunts of the gourmet-minded but, nevertheless, providing a good public service for late-night revellers, night-shift workers, and a variety of street lizards. There had been a stall at the foot of the Overgate, facing High Street, since before the last war. Another was to be found in Lindsay Street, just off the main thoroughfare. This one was owned by the well-known local baker J. Murdoch "Murdie" Wallace, who later went on to run a dance hall and whose symbols of success included a Rolls Royce and giant-sized cigars. Murdie's stall was a long, cream-coloured trailer which was hauled into position at ten each evening and then towed away again at around three in the morning. It did a steady trade in tea, coffee, hot dogs, mince rolls, egg rolls, and pies. It was claimed, in fact, that the first hot dogs in Scotland were sold from a similar stall in Dundee in the late Thirties, at a time when sausages inside rolls were all the rage in America. Murdie ran a tight ship in Lindsay Street for a varied clientele, which included Lords and Ladies, tramps and pedlars – ministers, doctors, solicitors, stockbrokers, and priests. To begin with many of the professional people preferred to remain incognito when they called at the stall. Ministers, for example, might wear mufflers to conceal their dog collars. But the regularity of their visits, and the friendly atmosphere behind the mobile counter, soon removed such inhibitions. Murdie was fond of recalling the night a smartly-suited gent crossed over to the stall from a chauffeur-driven limousine. Thinking he recognised the figure in the back seat he sauntered across himself with the hot dog order. Sure enough, the customer was Hector McNeil, Secretary of State for Scotland

WORTHIES

The Overgate has produced many worthies in its day. Before the First World War there was "Coffin Tam," the eccentric ironmonger who was said to have made and stored his own coffin in the back premises of his shop. At about the same time a formidable lady known as the "Iron Horse" frequented several of the pubs and could drink pint for pint with any navvy. Later on, just before the last war, David Ferguson was manager of Caledonian Tailors, next to Greenhill's the chemist. On a Saturday evening David would don one of the new coats for sale and pose as a dummy in the main window. Whenever a child started staring at him from the pavement he would stick out his tongue, whereupon the youngster would yell, "That manny's real." This would cause a crowd to gather. At that point the "dummy" would suddenly come to life and hold up a sale notice advertising the coat. "It's amazing how many garments we sold by this method," said David, looking back on his days as a "model." Another great character was Millie Carstairs who worked in one of the Overgate chip shops. After finishing work each day, shortly before one o'clock in the morning, she would make up a parcel of fish heads and other discarded cuts before heading for home in Bernard Street, Hawkhill. At exactly the same time cats from all directions would, as if by some secret signal, start gathering in the darkness under the clock in West Port. By the time Millie arrived between fifty and sixty cats were waiting patiently to be fed by the small woman in the blue trenchcoat and berry. Soon they were swirling round her legs as she distributed the fish. "It was a remarkable ritual," said a house-holder who lived there at the time. "It was uncanny how all these cats could time her arrival to the minute."

The Overgate

In earlier times

OUR LADY WARKSTAIRS

In early times the Overgate was occupied by the city's most prominent families, many of them captains of industry and leading citizens. It was a desirable residential area. This timber-fronted house – known as Our Lady Warkstairs and not much to look at by present-day standards – was built around 1450 at the foot of Overgate on the High Street, facing across to what would later be Crichton Street. Originally an almshouse and called Our Lady's Work – a reference to Dundee's patron saint, Mary – the Norman pillars supporting the front of the building formed an open piazza, within which open staircases led down to subterranean booths. This typical urban mansion of its period was a real mixter-maxter affair with hardly any two of the many rooms being on the same level, thus giving nine floors all linked by short flights of stairs. Later the interior was richly decorated in Queen Anne style. The house stood until 1879.

FAMOUS HOUSE

This was one of the most famous – and best-known – of the old Overgate houses, occupying a commanding position at the bottom left-hand corner of the thoroughfare, latterly across from Boots. Although considerably altered in appearance, it survived until the demolition orgy of the 1960's. Erected possibly towards the end of the 15th century as a tolbooth, its massive corner tower and corbelled bracketings gave it a fortress-like appearance appropriate to a building which, in its earlier days, guarded the western approaches to the city. This was possibly why General Monck commandeered it as his headquarters after capturing the town in 1651, an episode described in the following pages. Earlier that same year, during the unrest of the Civil War, a large number of royalist Scottish noblemen had taken refuge in Dundee. They included Francis, Earl of Buccleuch, who occupied this tower house in the Overgate, and it was there that his daughter, Anna, later to become Duchess of Buccleuch and Monmouth, was born in February 1651 – in the same space to be occupied three centuries later by the Sixty Minute Cleaners.

GENERAL MONCK

Dundee, strategically placed on the east coast of Scotland with fine port facilities and an attractive hinterland, was at one time considered a rich prize by various marauding armies. Indeed, it has been besieged, invaded, pillaged, ransacked, set on fire, and occupied more often than any other town in Scotland. And during these earlier centuries much of this violent action unfolded in the Overgate area, no more so than at the time of Dundee's famous sacking by General Monck in 1651. These were the years of civil war in Britain with Oliver Cromwell, the Lord Protector of England, in deadly combat against Charles I and seeking to subdue all those communities which supported the royalist cause. Dundee had displayed such tendencies and so Cromwell's army, under the generalship of George Monck, the 1st Duke of Albemarle, headed north for Dundee in its victorious sweep through Scotland.

There are many versions of how Monck finally took the city, most commonly that his forces merely had to slip through defences littered with the bodies of drunken guards. But the truth of the matter is much different – and, militarily at least, much more interesting. As Monck's army approached Dundee with a considerable force of nearly 6000 experienced troops, supported by artillery and horse, the defending garrison, augmented by reinforcements from Edinburgh, was confident of holding its ground with superior numbers in a town whose fortifications had only recently been strengthened. They had, however, failed to occupy either Broughty Castle or the Law and when Monck arrived on the outskirts, sometime before the end of July 1651, he promptly took possession of both these strategic positions. Both sides then invited each other to surrender and when these requests were duly ignored the battle for Dundee got under way.

Over the next three weeks attack and counter attack yielded no ground and finally Monck was forced to send to Stirling for two heavy mortars and introduce ten naval guns to supplement his own armour. Having by then pin-pointed the weakest part of the defences – the intelligence reports said to have been supplied by a town urchin slipping past the guards at night – the General proceeded to launch a fierce bombardment over several days. By the First of September two great breaches had been opened up in the city wall enabling Monck to send in a strong force of raiders, almost like commandos, followed up by 300 mounted dragoons. Everything went to plan and in a short time the English army had over-run the local garrison, surprising even two battalions of one regiment which were on parade in the High Street when the invaders suddenly appeared in their midst and cut them down. What followed was a scorched earth policy of slaughter and destruction. No mercy was shown by the victors because Monck, normally not given to wanton butchery, had seemingly been angered and humiliated by his earlier failure to take the town.

Amidst all this carnage the local governor, Sir Robert Lumsden, and some of his supporters had sought refuge in St. Mary's Tower which had been fortified and stocked with provisions and ammunition. For three days they held out, resisting capture by the use of heavy muskets from the ramparts of the Old Steeple, until eventually they were smoked down by bales of burning straw on the ground floor. When the governor and his party surrendered Monck ordered them to be treated with all honours due to an opposing leader. But while being marched into custody one of the officers shot the governor dead and ordered his men to kill the others. Lumsden's head was then displayed from St. Mary's Tower. Following the

capture of Dundee, during which the death roll rose to 1200, there was widespread pillaging. According to the rules of battle at that time a victorious commander seemingly had the right to allow his men to help themselves to whatever property they fancied for twenty-four hours. What was found in the houses of citizens, or "on their person," was the soldiers' lawful plunder, including horse equipment, money, and valuables. Monck's men certainly did well out of Dundee. Many wealthy people from Edinburgh had taken shelter in the town with everything they could carry and it was estimated that money and goods to the value of nearly £250,000 was commandeered by the invaders – said to be the most lucrative prize of any engagement throughout the civil war period. But the sixty ships captured in the harbour and sent south with other treasure were all lost at sea before even crossing the Bar of the Tay, either because of bad weather, indifferent seamanship, or excessive cargoes.

Monck remained in Dundee for only two months, establishing his headquarters in the corner tower house at the foot of the Overgate where Anna, Duchess of Buccleuch and Monmouth, had been born only months before. His garrison, however, stayed on for another eight years during which time 66 local women married the resident soldiers, giving birth to 250 children. In fact, there are likely to be descendants of Cromwell's soldiers walking about in Dundee to this very day. But it took over a century for the town to recover from this catastrophe and, although it finally managed to regain its prosperity, Dundee never restored its position as second burgh to Edinburgh.

ST. SALVADOR'S

One of the famous passageways in the early Overgate was St. Salvador's Close on the north side of the thoroughfare, running up to what later became the Howff. It took its name from one of the earliest altars established in the Parish Church of Dundee in dedication to St. Salvador. Indeed, the five tenements on each side of the close contributed annual rents to the upkeep of the altar, which was a common method of raising funds in these days for the maintenance of churches and their chaplains. Many of Dundee's leading merchants had their houses in St. Salvador's Close, including James Rollok who served several terms as Provost and was also responsible for the Customs of the burgh. Towards the end of the 15th century Exchequer Courts were often held in Dundee, demanding the presence of the King, then James IV, who, on these occasions, lodged with Provost Rollock in St. Salvador's Close. There is recorded that on such a royal visit on December 22, 1497, the Lord High Treasurer was commanded to make payment to the Provost in acknowledgement of his "digs." In these earlier centuries the Overgate lay at the heart of the ecclesiastical movement in Dundee. Within its greater area there stood a nunnery, monastery, a choristers' house for pre-Reformation church workers, the garden of the Franciscan Friars (the Howff), and various other houses accommodating chaplains who took the services in the local churches including, of course, the City Churches which still remain to this day. Another famous entry in the old Overgate was Methodist Close which ran parallel to Friars' Vennel, later to be renamed Barrack Street. This close had obvious associations with the Methodist movement in the city and contained a meeting house and chapel for members within one of its tenements.

MERCAT CROSS

One of the most powerful symbols of civic and business life in early Scotland was the Mercat Cross – a unicorn on top of a pillar, rising from a tower which stood on a graded plinth. It was round the Cross that much of the burgh's economic and administrative life revolved. It was the centre of trading – the "market-place" – and those who ran the town would meet within the tower and make all their important announcements, both local and national, from the roof of the tower itself. For example, when Mary Queen of Scots was in Dundee in 1565 the Privy Council had a proclamation made at the Cross warning the burgesses "against believing rumours that Her Majesty intended to subvert the national religion." The Mercat Cross also held the instruments of punishment – the jougs, the brank's bridle, the cucking stool, the pillory, the headsman's block, and the gallows – and it was here that offenders were brought to confess their crimes and be sentenced in public.

Dundee's Cross originally stood in the Seagate in the 14th century when that area was still the hub of the community. But when the town began expanding westwards into High Street, Nethergate, and Overgate the centre of trading moved there also and with it, in the middle of the 15th century, went the Mercat Cross. It remained at the west end of the High Street, at the foot of the Overgate, until 1777 when it was removed because of its obstruction to traffic. Later it reappeared near the front entrance of St. Mary's Tower and in 1874 was re-erected at the corner of Lindsay Street facing the Nethergate. Today the Mercat Cross can be seen in front of the City Churches – but without the original tower it is not a patch on the Cross that once dominated life in the ancient burgh.

LUCKENBOOTHS

Luckenbooths were a feature of early retail trading in Scotland and were to be found in various locations in Dundee, including the foot of the Overgate facing on to the High Street. When the town's principal merchants built their houses in the Middle Ages they often placed them back from the main thoroughfare with plots of land between their front door and the street. Latterly they utilised that land by erecting one-storey booths against the front of the houses – like lean-to's – thus enabling them to sell their merchandise to passers-by. These booths were roofed over and then shuttered for security, thereby making them lucken or locked booths. When these early houses were rebuilt they took in the ground occupied by the luckenbooths, which is why streets with booths on both sides of the road eventually became so narrow.

THE SIEGE

One of the many narrow passageways which intersected the tenementlands of the Overgate area from early days was Kirk Wynd, which ran from Thorter Row to East Kirk Style, later to be known as Tally Street. Kirk Wynd itself was also renamed latterly as Church Lane and at its corner with Thorter Row – where later stood the famous Cafe Royal Bar – there was once the mansion house of the Drummond family, the town's leading bakers, one of whose members, William Drummond, represented his craft for several years on the town council. They were pillars of respectability. In 1584, however, the Drummond house was the centre of a spectacular siege involving the Earl of Gowrie who had taken shelter there after being forced to flee his home, Ruthven Castle in Perth, after failing in a plot against King James VI, which became known as the Raid of Ruthven. The King's favourite henchmen, the Earl of Arran and the Duke of Lennox, had planned to seize Gowrie and a number of other Presbyterian nobles – and banish leading ministers of the Kirk – in an attempt to uphold Catholic authority. But Gowrie and his supporters, in a pre-emptive strike, lured the young monarch to Ruthven Castle on the pretence of offering him a spot of hunting – and then proceeded to keep him virtually under house arrest for the next ten months. When the King finally escaped their clutches he branded Gowrie a traitor. The Earl had then sought "digs" from the Drummonds on the understanding thar he was on his way into exile in France, but on the pretence of awaiting the arrival of his ship at Dundee he was secretly hoping to receive a signal from his followers – known as the Gowrie Conspirators – that would trigger another act of insurrection against the crown. Someone, however, had betrayed the plot to the Earl of Arran who promptly despatched Colonel William Stewart to Dundee with a hundred horsemen to arrest Gowrie. At the same time the Provost of Dundee, James Halyburton, was instructed to proclaim the errant Earl as a traitor at the Mercat Cross. The Colonel's squadron arrived in the early hours of April 16, 1584, and, having tracked their quarry to the Drummond residence – the location now occupied by Littlewoods Stores – called on Gowrie to give himself up. The troopers, however, were fired upon with such ferocity they were forced to retreat to a safe distance. Although the Earl and his supporters didn't have the strength to cut their way through the cordon of horsemen, and knowing they were for the chop anyway when finally captured, the fugitives were determined to go down with all guns firing.

Meanwhile the Colonel called up reinforcements in the shape of heavy cannons from ships lying in the harbour and proceeded to pound the Drummond mansion with an artillery barrage which caused a great commotion in the town. Crowds turned out to watch the siege move towards its climax. The psychological tactics and soothing talk employed in such situations nowadays hadn't been invented in the 16th century. It was all or nothing. Finally the bombardment breached the walls of the house and the conspirators were over-run by the King's men. Gowrie was taken before the Privy Council in Edinburgh for trial, found guilty of treason, and on May 2 met his death on the scaffold in the lee of Stirling Castle. Drummond's house had suffered much damage and one can only hope he was properly insured! In any event, the Drummond mansion continued in existence until being demolished, in a non-military fashion, in 1865.

WELLS

For centuries before people could turn on a tap in their house, water in Dundee – or anywhere else for that matter – was provided by a series of public wells, supplemented by a number of private wells sunk in backlands and closes. The Overgate Well originally stood at the corner of Tally Street, but was removed in 1828 to Mid Kirk Style nearby At that time water was also hawked round the streets by a fleet of twenty horse-drawn carts, the water caddies, as they were called, selling about a thousand gallons a day at a penny for ten gallons or a halfpenny per bucket. Women would jostle round their local well to fill their own pitchers as children frolicked beside the elaborate, stone-built fountain heads. But such scenes reflected anything but domestic bliss, as revealed in the following letter which appeared in the Dundee Courier in August, 1828: "Were you, sir, to witness the distress the poorer part of our community are put to for want of water, I am sure you would pity them. Mothers, of a morning, with their infants in their arms, half-dressed, carrying water not fit for a cow to drink – the aged, the infirm and the sickly, all are allowed to crawl as best they may to seek for the element so essential to their health and which they can obtain only in quantities limited and very impure." Indeed, much earlier – in 1799 – it was said that the town's water supply would "disgrace the meanest village in Britain." Under the Dundee Water Act of 1845 a private company provided the town's supply from Monikie and Stobsmuir, but it was not until the local authority took over the responsibility for water in the 1870's, utilising Lintrathen Loch and building Clatto Reservoir, that a start was made to establishing a proper, hygienic supply for the city. By 1874 Dundee's wells had been closed.

The Overgate

Back to the later years

STREET THEATRE

The Overgate was a natural setting for street theatre with its narrow, central passageway enclosed within a conglomeration of tenements of varying shapes and sizes. The lay-out provided a dramatic stage for the big event and none came bigger each year than Hogmanay. Revellers took over the Overgate, turning it into one massive, jostling crowd from end to end. A solid line of barrows stretched from Tay Street down to Reform Street. They were lit up by naphtha lamps and sold dressed herring, balloons, and fancy hats, the vendors all vying for custom by shouting and blowing trumpets. The din was terrible – but on New Year's eve no-one was really complaining. One of the personalities on this night of celebration was Kate Legget, described as the herring queen, whose barrow always occupied the stance at Boots corner. Anyone attempting to muscle in on her territory was unceremoniously evicted. On a more frequent basis the Overgate was also the setting for Dundee's famous "Monkey Parade." This was the affectionate description given to an event each Sunday evening in which hundreds of young men and women would promenade up and down the street in their own groups, mingling and exchanging gossip. This social ritual also provided an excellent opportunity for the lads and lasses to "weigh up the talent." Many a courtship leading to marriage began in this fashion.

Drama of a different sort was handled by the "midwives" – the women up every close who were capable of delivering a child. The baby would be laid at the side of the mother who was then given tea and toast until the official midwife arrived to cut the cord. "My mother did this all the time between the wars," remembered Margaret Mather, Dundee's present Citizen of the Year. "She also washed down and dressed the bodies of those who had just died for half-a-crown a time." The Overgate was also the scene of many demonstrations during the troubled economic years between the two world wars. In 1921, for example, there was rioting and looting in Dundee over the denial of unemployment benefit to married women whose husbands were already in receipt of this payment. Hundreds of demonstrators surged down the Overgate smashing shop windows on the way. Nellie Hanley, then only five, was standing with her mother on the pavement when a tin of corned beef or soup rolled across the road and landed at their feet. "In those days most women wore black knitted shawls," she recalled, "and meh mother bent down and put the tin under her shawl." The next minute they were being chased up a close by a Bobby on the back of a horse.

They managed to evade arrest by running upstairs to the plettie, from where they looked down on the horse and mounted policeman, both with their nostrils flaring but unable to reach them on high. At that time the rioting lasted for three days with most of those taking part being women who were desperate for food to sustain their children. "Eh think the men were scared," says Nellie today. In any event, the Parish Council decided to make relief available immediately without the usual investigations. Years later, in another demonstration which spread into the Overgate, a similar young girl also described the experience of being caught up with mounted police: "It was like all hell let loose. Oh my God! Now if you were in the way it didnae matter who you were, you just had had it. There was damned big horses comin' beltin' after ye … chasing the crowd, the sparks wir flying from hooves. Ah wis on the road t' hell, and that's something ah'll never forget (laughing), because it wis like a great big elephant t' me, o' what a size o' a horse. But ye know, we were only about eleven years old (laughing). Oh, it was frightening."

THE FIREMASTER

Captain James Sinclair Weir, Dundee's distinguished firemaster for 33 years – from 1904 until 1937 – was a familiar figure in the Overgate through the various fires he attended over the years in that part of the city. He was a kindly man who always carried a few coins in his pocket for the beggars who would invariably approach him at the scene of an outbreak. "He'll just drink it," was the comment once made by a colleague who had witnessed one of these cash transfers. "Yes, I know," said the Captain, "but it will make him happy for a wee while." On other occasions when a house had been badly damaged by fire and the tenant had been unable to afford insurance cover he would arrange to have a few pounds sent on to them. The Firemaster was able to relate very easily to the hardship he saw in the Overgate and elsewhere, having himself had to rough it in the earlier part of his life. He belonged to a small village near Dunnet Bay in Caithness and went to sea as a cook's boy at the tender age of eleven, sailing to many parts of the world. He eventually joined the fire service in Edinburgh, rose to become a lieutenant, and then, in 1904, was appointed Firemaster of Dundee with the rank of captain. Soon his exploits as a fire fighter had turned him into a legendary figure. He won two medals for gallantry, one of them the so-called "Fireman's V.C." for rescuing two Lascar seamen from the burning hold of a jute ship. He was a fearless man whose skill in containing fires led to the belief that he could even find water in a desert. Indeed, some youngsters in the Overgate composed a skipping jingle in his honour: "Fire in the Lochee Road boys, fire in the Lochee Road. Send for Captain Weir boys, send for Captain Weir." He was also a popular figure with the Press. On one occasion when a large mansion was ablaze in the Carse of Gowrie the owner banned reporters from the scene.

But the Firemaster, sympathising with the newsmen, simply equipped one of them with a helmet and hose so that he could get near enough to describe the fire and the damage it had caused. He was a bit of a scribe himself, writing a column in his native John O'Groats Journal to keep northern readers in touch with their kinsfolk in the Dundee area. Captain Weir was still in service when he collapsed and died at the age of 66 in 1937, having been retained beyond the age limit to organise the local Auxiliary Fire Service which would be implemented in the event of war. His funeral was one of the biggest seen in the city for many years. The service was conducted in the engine room of the Bell Street Fire Station with mourners present from nearly every brigade in Scotland, and many beyond, reflecting his prominence outwith the city which had led him to become President of the Association of Professional Fire Brigade Officers of the British Empire in 1930-31. The coffin, bearing his helmet and axe, was mounted on a big, six-wheeler engine and the cortege then led by the police pipe band to Balgay Cemetery.

The streets were lined with people paying their last respects, many of them from the Overgate where he had been such a popular figure. The funeral took 35 minutes to pass. The throb of the fire engine which had carried him to hundreds of outbreaks was the only sound to break the silence as the coffin was lowered into the grave. Even when off duty the Captain had been ever-ready for action, his fire fighting gear always being carried in his car. He also had a special buzzer fitted to his pew at church so that in the event of a call-out during the Sunday morning service he could be summoned by a fireman pressing a button on the kirk door. Firemen still speak about Captain Weir to this day.

SHOPS

The Overgate's popularity rested heavily on the character of its shops. They came in all shapes and sizes – a step up to some, a step down to others – all jammed intimately together in higgledy-piggledy fashion but creating a home-spun, friendly atmosphere which made that part of the city a great favourite for family outings. Here you could find virtually anything you wanted. In the early days there was Palmer's Rock Shop near Long Wynd with crook-handled, red-striped, candy walking sticks dangling on cords in brightly-lit windows. Youngsters also made a bee-line for Sammy Lee's fantastic toyshop with its vast range of cheap, German-made toys. A host of other celebrated names also traded along the main thoroughfare. There was Wilkie, the butcher; Petrie, the jeweller; the shoe shops of Birrell, Patterson, and Saxone; Keith Scott, the draper; the "Bonanza" dress shop; Wallace, the baker; Reilly's Amusement Arcade; Fagan, the broker; ironmongers Kirk and Coutts; Massey and Lipton the grocers; Durham, the printers – and a mass of others. Those shops which disappeared in the redevelopment of the Overgate included the popular dress parlour of Miss Peebles, at the corner of Tally Street and Nethergate. The Overgate had one of the smallest shops in town – the Tom Thumb Fruit Bazaar. It sat below pavement level, a couple of steps taking you into the cramped interior past one tiny window. The fruit and veg. was all stacked against the walls inside. Pavement displays were not recommended. Mary Knox, now 83, worked in the shop for several years during the last war. "Three customers in the place and you were full," she remembered with a smile. "It was like working in a doll's house – but it was great fun." At one time, many centuries before, the Overgate housed the Scottish Mint. Later it was the shops that made the money in this part of Dundee.

BARBERS

The retail section of the Overgate would not have been complete without its barber shops, the red and white poles like giant sticks of rock heralding their presence among the jumble of other premises. Possibly the most renowned of these establishments was run by one of Dundee's enduring characters, Pat Fletcher, who became a legend in his fifty years in the famous street. For Pat was much more than a gent's hairdresser. He was also a town councillor, magistrate, orator, debater, and philosopher. His small shop became a favourite meeting place for the politically inclined – an extension almost of the town council which he joined in 1913 and remained a member until 1931. Many a debate on local issues held the floor, almost taking precedence over shaves and haircuts. Joining the Independent Labour Party as a young man, Pat became embroiled in much controversy during the First World War through his staunch stance as a pacifist. By 1932 he had become a member of the Labour Party and was now a kenspeckle figure on public platforms all over Britain, his fiery oratory attracting large audiences. In Scotland he cycled to many of his public meetings, sometimes arriving breathless but always able to get people to their feet. He never sought a Parliamentary seat although being offered, but declining, an invitation to stand for a Birmingham constituency. Pat was 90 when he died in April, 1963. In stark contrast to the timeless atmosphere of Pat Fletcher's shop, there came later a quite different type of hairdressing establishment to the Overgate. This was Gibson's, a high-speed barber with seven chairs where the standard short-back-and-sides and a bit off the top took only as long as a brief discussion on the weather that day. Speed here was of the essence. Appropriately, the assistants were often known as the "bonus barbers."

LIVING IN THE OVERGATE

Jane Burnett, the daughter of a factory worker, and Anna, Duchess of Buccleuch and Monmouth, who was a high-ranking member of the aristocracy, have one thing in common: they were born in the same house in the Overgate – the famous turreted tenement at the foot, facing on to High Street. Anna was delivered there in February, 1651, with a silver spoon in her mouth. Nearly 300 years later – in 1920 – Jane was also born there, one stair up in the same building, but without any of Anna's built-in privileges. By the time Jane appeared on the scene No. 8 Overgate had long since ceased to be a fashionable address. Indeed, living in the Overgate during its last hundred years or so, in the midst of much slum property, carried a certain stigma. Jane found this out to her cost and deeply resented the slur. When, for example, she left Harris Academy in 1938 she encountered great difficulty in finding a job, despite being well-qualified with "Highers." "I knew it was my address that was putting employers off," she explained, "and at one stage my aunt suggested that I used her address when posting off applications. But I was determined to stick to No. 8 Overgate and in the end I did find work as a shorthand-typist." It was the same in the jute mills. A woman coming from the Overgate was also apt to be looked down upon. Apart from this, however, Jane Burnett had a happy upbringing between the two world wars in her two-roomed house in one of Dundee's less reputable quarters. "I loved the atmosphere of the place," she said, "and we didn't think it was down-market at all. There were many interesting shops at our end of the Overgate – Liptons, Wilkie the butcher, Roy the fruiterer, Jessie Mitchell the grocer – and with lots of closes and backlands it was a great place for playing in, particularly at hide and seek."

HORSE ARTIST

One of Britain's top experts in drawing horses – particularly working horses – produced his highly-acclaimed equine studies from studios located at the foot of the Overgate, overlooking the High Street and next door to General Monck's headquarters. It was from here that Bill McCail launched his one-man exhibitions in many parts of the country. His drawings, wonderfully evocative of the horse's power, elegance, and dedication to work, hang on walls all over the world. One of his studies was bought by the Queen Mother. Bill belonged to West Hartlepool, County Durham, and after school became a deck-boy on a paddle tug-boat and then an apprentice joiner in a shipyard. But he later turned to art and arrived in Dundee to work as an illustrator with D. C. Thomson, drawing for the boys' papers and women's magazines, just as his brother Jack had done before him. In 1940 he branched out on his own as a freelance artist, supplying comic strips and scripts for a publisher in London. Later he became an artists' agent and established a national art-agency in Dundee, channelling the work of many Scottish artists and script writers to newspapers, magazines, and book publishers nation-wide. In 1948 he moved his agency to the Overgate area, occupying a centuries-old former house with low ceilings and an outside staircase alongside the Maryfield and Downfield tram stops. It was then that he turned his own artistic skills to a long-time interest in horses, mastering their anatomy by drawing every evening in the stables of the L.M.S. Railway Company in South Union Street and observing them at work each day as they hauled heavy loads of jute up through the city from the sheds at Dundee Harbour. He also enjoyed drawing at race meetings and circuses. Bill McCail gave the horse the dignity it deserved. He died in 1974 at the age of 72.

FANNY WRIGHT

Frances "Fanny" Wright was in the same mould as Margaret Thatcher – a tough, uncompromising woman with the courage of her own convictions; the possessor of a sharp brain and boundless energy; a person both admired and detested for the way she wanted to reorganise society; a lady who was very definitely not for turning. Fanny was born in 1795 in Miln's Buildings at 136 Nethergate, a building which still stands on the south side of this main thoroughfare between Marketgait and South Tay Street. Her father, James Wright, was a linen merchant, scholar, and radical activist who supported the aims and achievements of the French Revolution. At that time – the early 1790's – Dundee was a city riddled with poverty where workers had few rights and the wealthy elite ruled the roost. Living close to the Overgate, Fanny saw the consequences of this multi-deprivation for herself, a childhood experience she never forgot in a life that was to be dedicated to the abolition of slavery and the cause of "women's lib" in the new, independent land of America where she first took her reforming zeal in 1818. The young Dundee woman had good – if rather masculine – looks, a commanding presence, powerful oratory, and money in the bank. She launched an experimental community at Nashoba in Tennessee where, having purchased a number of slaves, she set them to work under supervision until they had earned enough to buy their freedom. But the project failed, largely because of its location on 2000 acres of miserable swampland. She also campaigned against organised religion, conventional morality, and the traditional structure of marriage, proposing that all children from the age of two should be taken from their parents and raised without frills in boarding schools. Despite much outraged opposition, Fanny Wright, born within sight and sound of the Overgate, wrote herself into the pages of American social history.

JEANNIE GALL

earlier training. "Ma" Gall was invariably dressed in black with a pilgrim's bonnet and lived in the locality herself. On dark evenings her presence in the street was picked out in a pool of light from a lamp at the end of a pole held by one of her young assistants. Her religious services were usually kept under observation by the beat policeman who would keep troublemakers at bay. On one occasion a local drunk, who didn't have a tooth in his head and was nicknamed "Big Chief Cave in the Mouth," became so enthralled with Jeannie's singing that he suddenly shouted a request. "Gie wiz the Old Rugged Cross, Miss Gall," he demanded. The missionary gave him a look of disdain. "This is not a music hall young man," she retorted. "This is the House of God." Jeannie also held indoor services in the city and was widely respected as a tireless worker for the poor and homeless until becoming bedridden with arthritis in 1971. She died seven years later at the age of 80.

The Overgate undoubtedly had a bad name, the blame for which lay very largely with those who visited the area. It had been denounced from pulpit and temperance platform as "a sordid sink of squalor, drink, and human degradation." Not surprisingly, therefore, it was a place well targeted by those who sought to convert the sinners – evangelists, revivalists, and sundry preachers. Hymn singers were also in attendance, joined often by drunks who sang their heads off until thirst drove them back into the pubs once more. It was in this fertile setting for moral change that Jeannie Gall, a roving missionary, did much of her work. Blind from youth, she held regular open-air services, playing a portable organ and singing sweetly with a voice which bore all the hallmarks of an

BEEFCAN CLOSE

At one time the Overgate had a large network of closes – Argyll, Highland, Matthew, Yeaman, Methodist, Guthrie, Boyack, Rodger, St. Salvador, Mint Close, and so on. But latterly there was one particular close which, although never being officially named, was deeply-rooted in the folklore of the area. It was called the Beefcan Close. This was an entry next to the British and Argentine Meat Company – also known as the River Plate Meat Shop – at No. 105, between Barrack Street and North Lindsay Street. This butcher's shop sold large quantities of corned beef imported from South America in big tins. When these cans were emptied they were piled up for collection at the mouth of the close outside, which soon acquired the name of Beefcan Close. This spot became so well-known, in fact, that it featured in a famous Overgate song all of its own:

Now as I went up the Overgate, I met Jemima Ross,
An' she winked at me wi' the tail o' her e'e,
In the middle o' the Beefcan Close.

Chorus
Ricky doo dum day, doo dum day,
Ricky-dicky doo dum day.

I asked her who she stayed with,
An' she said it was Mistress Bruce,
An' after that I got an invitation
up tae her hoose.

When I went up the close that nicht,
The stairs wis awfy dark,
So I took my money fae my inside pooch,
an' I tied it tae the tail o' my sark.

When I went in the hoose that nicht,
I ower tae the chair sat doon,
But she winked at me wi' the tail o' her e'e,
An' she says, "Come ben the room."

Now a' that nicht I dreamt I wis in,
The airms o' Jemima Ross,
But when I woke up I was on ma back,
In the middle o' the Beefcan Close.

Now a' ye lads an' lassies here,
When ye gang oot for a lark,
Jist be like me when ye're on a spree,
Tie the money tae the tail o' yer sark.

An' now my song is ended here,
I hope you enjoyed it well,
An' when you go up the Overgate,
See an' enjoy yersel'.

SCHOOL

The Overgate had no factories, no cinemas, and no dance halls as such. But it did have a well-known school – St Andrew's Roman Catholic Primary, walled in just behind the play area at the junction with Long Wynd. It opened as a girls' school in 1871, but later took in boys as well, before finally falling to a demolition order in the late 50's. Many former pupils, particularly those from the earlier years, nurture sharp memories of a disciplined regime long since gone from the educational scene. When Mary Lannen, now 84, was a pupil at St. Andrew's during the First World War one of the Sisters would stand at the front door with her strap every morning. "Anyone who arrived late was given a whack before they even crossed the threshold," she remembered with a grimace. And Mary Brooksbank, who became a poet

and campaigner for workers' rights, had this to say in one of her books about her time at St. Andrew's: "The filth from the water closets littered the playground, due to the bad or primitive nature of the plumbing system. The Liberal government of that time had passed an Act providing for school dinners, but this was a farce since all we got was a half bowl of watery soup, and for this we had to pay a penny a week." Tom McPherson, however, enjoyed his time there during the last war. "Going to school in the Overgate was always interesting because you were surrounded by all these intriguing wee shops and there was always plenty to see as you went to and fro. And I'll never forget one of the teachers, Sister Mary Michael, gathering up her skirts and playing football with us in the playground."

The Overgate

As it might have been

PLAN ONE – THOMSON

The Overgate had long been recognised as a priority case for redevelopment and, being the most central and busiest of all the precincts, its scars were there for everyone to see. There was no way you could sweep the Overgate under the carpet. Between 1910 and 1952, therefore, three plans were prepared for its reincarnation. The first of these was drawn up by the city engineer and architect, James Thomson, who has been described as "the most under-rated figure in the history of Scottish town planning." In his scheme of central improvements, which incidentally included a grandiose civic centre on land reclaimed from Earl Grey Dock, he suggested the following measures to create a new Overgate:

Straighten and widen the Overgate along its whole length.

Demolish the entire bottom part on the south side right up to Tally Street and landscape the site with gardens and fountain.

Remove the buildings between Tally Street and Lindsay Street to allow for the expansion northwards of the grounds attached to the City Churches.

Rebuild most of the north side from High Street up to Tay Street.

In his report to the Town Council in August 1910, Thomson pulled no punches: "The condition of a large proportion of the properties, and the narrowness of the Overgate, demand that something should be done.

Many of the tenements of dwelling houses are beyond repair. Improvements, so-called, have been and are still being carried out on the properties, but these can only be regarded as temporary, as the only satisfactory method of treatment lies in demolition. Properties of an inferior kind abut on both sides for the greater part of its length, and in the rear of the front properties are buildings in such a state of congestion as to provide a density of 400 persons per acre, which compares with about 36 persons per acre for the whole city, while at some parts there is not even sufficient space to allow for the erection of modern sanitary conveniences. Overgate is one of the busiest of the thoroughfares which converge towards High Street. It is about 480 yards in length, the carriageway is 13 feet wide at its narrowest part, the footpaths are at some points as narrow as four feet, and it is altogether unsuited for either the pedestrian or the vehicular traffic of the present day." By removing the conglomeration of buildings to the north and east of the City Churches and St. Mary's Tower, Thomson saw the enhancement of Dundee's greatest medieval treasure as part of the city's grand new architectural image. In particular, demolishing the entire bottom part of the Overgate on the south side from the High Street to Tally Street and landscaping that triangular stretch of open ground, instead of filling it with new buildings, was a bold, imaginative step. And by widening the Overgate to 70 feet he proposed routing the Blackness tram right through its middle, thus providing a more direct link to the city centre. Had his vision been translated into action Dundee would have become the Paris of the North. As it transpired, the First World War put paid to his plan – to say nothing of the colossal cost involved – and after hostilities ended Dundee had greater economic priorities than a fancy, new Overgate and other central improvements.

PLAN TWO – ADAMS

It wasn't until 1936, as Britain was slowly emerging from the Depression, that Dundee Town Council moved again to tackle what Lord Provost John Phin described at the time as "one of the blackest spots of the city." They appointed Dr Thomas Adams, a London town planning consultant with an international reputation, to create a new Overgate. The plan he submitted the following year was, he said, designed to make the Overgate the most distinguished street in Dundee. His report went on: "... The extended civic and business centre thus obtained would be in size, and could be in dignity, artistic quality and adaptation to modern needs, equal to that of any city." He proposed:

A straight, wide street on a new alignment from the junction of High Street and Reform Street and ending at a large traffic circle in the vicinity of Long Wynd.

The bottom part of the old Overgate on the south side up to Tally Street to be permanently cleared of all buildings.

Shops to be provided on two levels with access stairs, bridges and arcaded side-walks.

The Adams Plan was dominated by the needs of future traffic growth and circulation. To this end it proposed five roads radiating from the impressive roundabout at the western end of Overgate. These would connect with the Nethergate, South Tay Street, South Ward Road, West Port, and, of course, the Overgate itself. The demolition of the foot of the Overgate up to Tally Street was also to provide for greater vehicular space. Although not segregating traffic and pedestrians in the new precinct, the plan intended to create ample safe space for those on foot with sufficient car parking on streets and at the rear of buildings. It was proposed that as far as practicable the professional centre of the city would be located in the vicinity of the new traffic circle. The main shopping frontages would run from the bottom of the Overgate on the north side up to Lindsay Street and then south on the west side of Lindsay Street, to the Nethergate. The buildings up to Barrack Street would have arcaded sidewalks.

The plan also had interesting proposals for The Howff, Dundee's ancient burial ground abutting the northern edge of the Overgate: "The Howff should be developed into a rest park, removing the upright monumental stones and relaying them flat in well arranged groups. They would thus remain as memorials, and there would be no disturbance of the graves. Where stones were in a partly perished condition they would be replaced with smaller stones of durable material. The effect would be to improve the memorial character of the graveyard and give it a pleasing appearance as a small park. If well planned and provided with additional trees and shrubs it would add to the amenities of the centre of the city and provide a beautiful rest park where it is much needed. A shelter should be erected and a formal garden laid out in the centre, the existing trees being preserved as far as possible ... an effort might be made to secure private funds for carrying out such a scheme." The report concluded that it would take 30 to 40 years to complete the new Overgate, although a considerable part of the scheme could be carried out immediately. Towards the end of 1937 the Town Council adopted the Adams Plan. But one man was to prevent its execution – Adolf Hitler. For the second time, the outbreak of war frustrated the city's ambitious plans.

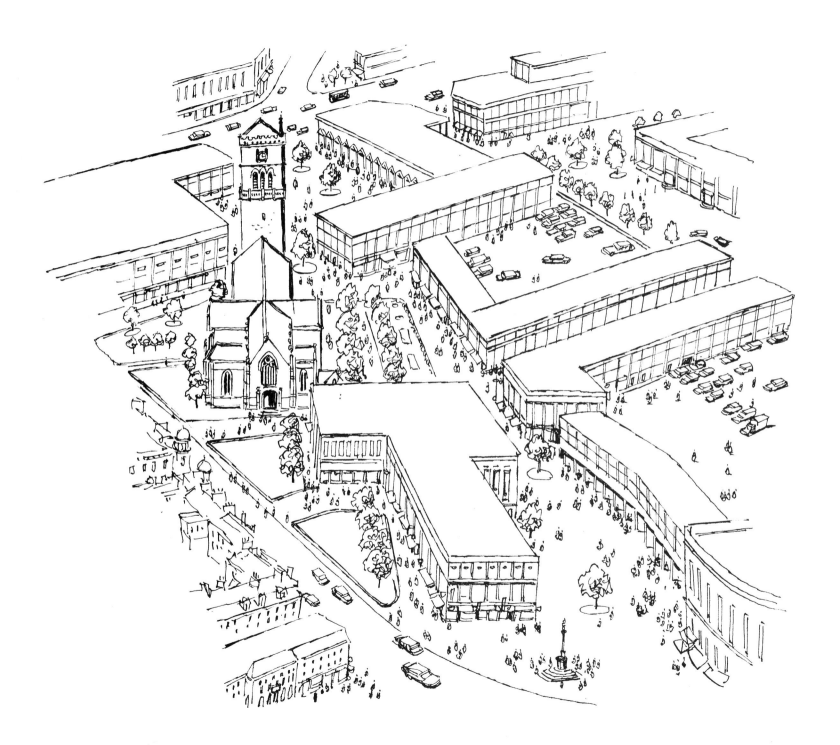

PLAN THREE – DOBSON CHAPMAN

By 1950 the Overgate had become a serious and embarrassing problem for the City Fathers, to say nothing of the dire conditions it continued to impose upon the many people who continued to live and work there. And so in that year W. Dobson Chapman and Partners, of Macclesfield, Yorkshire, were asked to prepare a comprehensive survey report and advisory plan for the redevelopment of the Overgate and other central areas of the city. Pointing out that very few changes had taken place in the city centre since the previous century, the planning consultants made the following observations: "The very scale of the city's redevelopment problems … is sufficient to daunt even the stout-hearted … Adequate solutions must be found if the city is to thrive, and they can be found, for the tempo of change in the immediate future is likely to be such as to make seemingly ambitious proposals a practical proposition… The deterioration of much of the older property in the central area of the city, the need to make adequate provision for increased road traffic, and for the cultural, recreational, and service requirements of a great commercial and regional centre … offers a great opportunity in compliance with recent legislation, for the preparation of a Town Planning Scheme. The scheme, while preserving all that is worthy of retention from the past, would discard the obsolescent and outworn parts, so that, by gradual stages the City of Dundee could be remodelled to provide a more satisfactory and worthwhile environment for its citizens." As far as the Overgate was concerned it was decided that the whole area between Reform Street and Long Wynd should be redeveloped as an extensive shopping precinct, together with a cinema between the north side of the Overgate and Bank Street, although none of this would involve the wholesale demolition of property. Many of the buildings were, of course, to be replaced but the plan allowed for the retention of some, notably at the junction of Overgate and Barrack Street, and further vetting of others before finally deciding whether to knock them down. But where the Dobson Chapman Plan broke new ground compared to the previous schemes was the provision it made for the complete segregation of the pedestrian and the motor vehicle and for the servicing of all shops and commercial premises from the rear. The report continued: "By the continuance of the existing garden development round the City Churches… it will be possible to retain and indeed enhance the historic character of this area of the city giving a personal character to the shopping area and at the same time setting off to better advantage the historical and architecturally unique mass of the combined City Churches and visually linking them with the very heart of the city. This conception is further developed by the opening out of the western end of this section of the Overgate into a pedestrian 'Place' surrounded by shops and dominated by the Steeple Church." It was this plan that undoubtedly had a very great influence on the eventual lay-out of the new Overgate, as drawn up by the Murrayfield Real Estate Company and subsequently promoted by the Town Council in September 1958, approved by the Secretary of State in August 1960, and starting to rise from the ashes of the old in October 1961. It had taken over fifty years from the first Thomson Plan in 1910 to begin the physical rebuilding of the Overgate.

JAMES THOMSON

Had Dundee been redeveloped in the vision of James Thomson, the city engineer and architect in the first part of this century, it would have been endowed with a fine, landscaped central area and a legacy of impressive civic buildings. Apart from an attractive, new Overgate, his 1910 Scheme of Central Improvements envisaged a magnificent civic centre on the in-filled sites of the Earl Grey and King William Docks; a huge circular covered market behind The Pillars Town House in the High Street, capable of accommodating 10,000 people; a widening and general improvement of both Crichton Street and Union Street, with South Union Street becoming a tree-lined boulevard leading to the Esplanade and an improved view of the river. Thomson was certainly a town planner before his time. In the event his grandiose blueprint for a rejuvenated city was never implemented because of the intervention of the First World War and the gradual economic decline of Dundee in the Twenties and Thirties. Thomson,

however, still left many grand buildings and much innovation behind to remind us of his considerable creative impact on the city. There are the outstanding Renaissance libraries at Blackness and Coldside (designed by his son Frank), followed later by those at St. Roque's and Ward Road; the garden city-type municipal housing scheme at Logie (the first in Europe to have a district central heating system) and the model for several others, including Craigiebank. One of his finest projects was the Kingsway ring road round the north of Dundee, a dual carriageway with a grassed central reservation stretching from Invergowrie in the west to the Arbroath Road at Craigiebank in the east. Constructed over a period of many years between the two world wars, it was yet another example of James Thomson's uncanny anticipation of public need, in this case the inexorable growth of road transport. He died in 1927 at the age of 75.

The Overgate

Demolition and after

RENEWAL

Although the final plan for the new Overgate wasn't approved by the Scottish Secretary until August 1960, Dundee Corporation had taken the cast-iron decision in January 1956 that, come what may, the redevelopment of the city's biggest eyesore was definitely going ahead. The Council had been gradually acquiring property in the Overgate throughout the years and was now in a strong position to dictate the timetable of events. In March 1957 – two-and-a-half years before a developer had even been appointed to the project – the first of the bulldozers moved into the Overgate to begin the biggest demolition programme ever seen in the central area of a Scottish city. Buildings at the corner of Overgate, Tally Street, and Mid Kirk Style, were brought tumbling down as a curtain-raiser to a massive clearance operation which was to continue over the next ten years. The developer finally selected was the Murrayfield Real Estate Company whose chairman, Field Marshal Sir Claude Auchinleck, had commanded the desert army in North Africa at the start of the last war. Three hundred years before it had been another general – Cromwell's George Monck – who had also taken a hand in the reshaping of the Overgate. But whereas Monck's role had been one of destructive invader, Auchinleck was bent only on peacetime reconstruction. His company was to redevelop the precinct in three stages:

Phase One. Starting at the west end of the site this would provide an arcade of 49 shop units and a long, six-storey slab block creating nearly 40,000 square feet of office space and a 60-bedroom hotel.

Phase Two. Based on a twin-level pedestrian precinct round the City Churches, this would give 26 units, two stores, and rooftop parking. The upper level of the shopping section would be a continuation of the shopping arcade in Phase One.

Phase Three. Centred on the High Street, this would comprise a multi-storey office block with another 30 units and two department stores on two levels, with an arcade linking High Street to the City Churches.

When the Murrayfield company swung into action in February, 1961, demolition was stepped up to make way for the construction of the first phase. That started in October the same year and wasn't completed until the end of 1963 – nine months behind schedule. The delay had been caused by site flooding, labour disputes, and Siberian winter conditions. The flooded foundations of the Angus Hotel was a particular problem, described at the time as an area of "running sand" which had not been detected by trial bores. De-watering plant was operated round the clock and work on the site came to a halt for 17 weeks while the foundations were drained and redesigned. Popular theory pointed to the water coming from the ancient Scouringburn which for centuries had run just north of the site, but such speculation was discounted by various experts. In any event the huge pond that formed in the foundations of the hotel proved a major attraction for Dundonians watching their city take on a new shape. The second phase was finished in 1966. By then the demolition of the bottom part of the Overgate had got under way for the final section of the development and now some of Dundee's oldest buildings were disappearing in a cloud of dust. By 1969 the massive project had been completed and the new Overgate had risen from the ashes of the old.

SOLE SURVIVORS

In all this "clean sweep" demolition of the Overgate only St. Mary's Tower and the City Churches remained untouched, standing defiantly all alone as everything around them was cast into oblivion. These places of worship had, of course, received much mauling in stormier times centuries before, although the Tower itself had always managed to survive. Now, freed from the clutter of adjoining, derelict properties, this ecclesiastical enclave was about to enjoy a new prominence on the local landscape.

NEW OVERGATE

When the new Overgate was finally unveiled it was hailed with great enthusiasm in various quarters – "a showpiece development giving a spacious, well-designed layout free of traffic which allows relaxed shopping in congenial surroundings," was how it was described in the official communique. People certainly flocked to Dundee's new retail wonderland, at that time the popular answer to the shopping needs of inner city areas. But the character of the original Overgate had entirely disappeared, as this frontal view of its replacement from the High Street end amply bears out. The atmosphere of the old place had gone forever, along with the traffic and houses which had once made the Overgate a vibrant, living area by night as well as by day. Now it was a functional stretch of impersonal concrete where the shutters were pulled down at closing time each evening.

NEW OVERGATE

Commercially, the twin-deck lay-out of shops was a great success in the early years – although, sadly, many of the previous Overgate shopkeepers found themselves unable to take premises in the new precinct despite an agreement between the Corporation and the developers that they should be offered reasonable accommodation. Indeed, it was estimated at the time that 60 per cent of shops had ceased trading altogether when having to vacate their old property. Gradually, however, the west end of the new development found itself out in the cold, too far away from the new and more modern enclosed shopping malls which had opened later in the Wellgate and other central areas, along with out-of-town retail parks and, latterly, the Waterfront development. The new Overgate was no longer the in-place. Refurbishment was clearly needed.

LOOKING AHEAD

This (below) is a close up view of the new central section as you would approach it from the Nethergate entering the pedestrian precinct between the City Churches and Littlewoods Store, the area previously occupied by Tally Street. Here you get a better look at the new enclosed stairway and lift at the east end of this section. The Marketgait entrance to the Overgate would also take on a new look. This, too, would be glazed over, incorporating a wind break feature which would help to eliminate the wind tunnel effect in that part of the development. Greater comfort for the shopper is the overall theme.

LOOKING AHEAD

Talk of remodelling the Overgate as a major retail centre has at long last been replaced by action. Plans had not been finalised when this book was published but a basic, £4 million renovation programme is already under way. As seen from these official artist's impressions, this plan envisages the exposed top deck of the long central section behind the City Churches (above) being covered over by an attractive glazed canopy. The concrete balcony would be replaced by traditional cast iron railings, thus opening up the view from ground level, and new staircases would be installed at either end together with a scenic lift to serve the various levels. Improved paving and lighting would be introduced throughout.

LOOKING AHEAD

This is how the development would look from the foot of Reform Street with a new canopied entrance enhancing the main access. The external concrete cladding on Littlewoods Store, which has caused much adverse comment, would be overlaid with attractive masonry softer on the eye. Other proposals for this end of the precinct include the removal of the existing concrete upstand walls at the staircase. These would be replaced with traditional cast iron decorative railings and improved lighting. The existing central stair would be removed to enable the lower area to be opened up and the escalator upgraded with mirror glass balustrading. It is now difficult to realise that this was once the foot of the old Overgate with General Monck's headquarters and various other medieval houses alongside looking out over the High Street. We emphasise, however, that all these changes represent a minimum new-look for the Overgate. But at the end of the day, redevelopment on a much more ambitious scale by the centre's owners, TBI plc, could provide Dundee with a new central precinct of impressive proportions.

The Overgate

Epilogue

JAMES BOYD

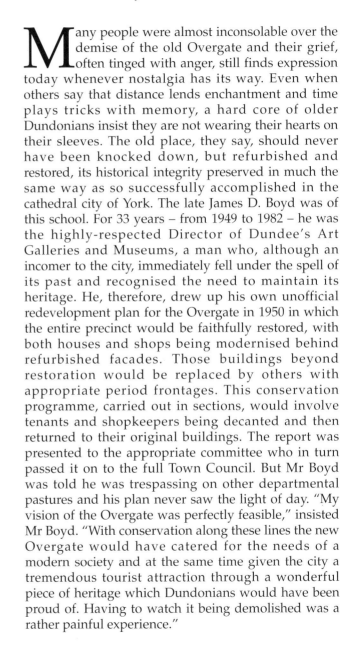

Many people were almost inconsolable over the demise of the old Overgate and their grief, often tinged with anger, still finds expression today whenever nostalgia has its way. Even when others say that distance lends enchantment and time plays tricks with memory, a hard core of older Dundonians insist they are not wearing their hearts on their sleeves. The old place, they say, should never have been knocked down, but refurbished and restored, its historical integrity preserved in much the same way as so successfully accomplished in the cathedral city of York. The late James D. Boyd was of this school. For 33 years – from 1949 to 1982 – he was the highly-respected Director of Dundee's Art Galleries and Museums, a man who, although an incomer to the city, immediately fell under the spell of its past and recognised the need to maintain its heritage. He, therefore, drew up his own unofficial redevelopment plan for the Overgate in 1950 in which the entire precinct would be faithfully restored, with both houses and shops being modernised behind refurbished facades. Those buildings beyond restoration would be replaced by others with appropriate period frontages. This conservation programme, carried out in sections, would involve tenants and shopkeepers being decanted and then returned to their original buildings. The report was presented to the appropriate committee who in turn passed it on to the full Town Council. But Mr Boyd was told he was trespassing on other departmental pastures and his plan never saw the light of day. "My vision of the Overgate was perfectly feasible," insisted Mr Boyd. "With conservation along these lines the new Overgate would have catered for the needs of a modern society and at the same time given the city a tremendous tourist attraction through a wonderful piece of heritage which Dundonians would have been proud of. Having to watch it being demolished was a rather painful experience."

JAMES PAUL

The case in favour of redevelopment is put by Professor James Paul, former Head of the School of Architecture, University of Dundee. He writes: "After the 1939-45 war many of our cities, badly damaged by enemy bombing, faced massive rebuilding programmes. At the same time consideration had to be given to the replacement of outdated properties in town centres, like the Overgate in Dundee. In all this, requirements for new shopping trends and commercial use of property – plus the anticipated growth of the motor vehicle – had to be rethought. The emphasis was on creating new sustainable developments and to facilitate this renewal in Scotland the Town and Country Planning Act of 1947 gave local authorities the power to acquire land and buildings and produce detailed development plans. The Overgate fell into this category, having in many ways outlived its usefulness. Not only was it decaying behind its facades, but its heavy stone and timber construction did not adapt to the large plan requirements of rapidly changing commercial uses. It is comparatively easy to romanticise about the past in terms of building without giving due thought to the social and economic considerations prevailing when they were conceived. The fabric of buildings can rapidly decay and the functions for which they were built become outmoded and cease to equate with social progress. Besides which, the preservation costs of old buildings can be prohibitive. Buildings can also be said to reflect the era in which they were built but historically, particularly in urban areas, their form and function was often dictated by a few people of influence who, in many cases, were not necessarily reflecting the needs of society at large but promoting their own limited requirements. In the case of the new Overgate decisions were made by democratically elected members of the Town Council and can therefore be said to have reflected the opinions of the majority of the electorate. The old place simply had to go."

ACKNOWLEDGEMENTS

The authors gratefully acknowledge the help given to them by various departments of the former Dundee District Council – Planning, Local History, and City archivist – and to D. C. Thomson & Co. Ltd. Our thanks are also due in no small measure to community historian Graham R. Smith; the late James D. Boyd, former Director of Art Galleries and Museums; Professor James Paul, former Head of the School of Architecture, University of Dundee; and to Tom and Simon McPherson for their pictorial guidance on St. Andrew's Primary School. We are indebted as well to TBI plc, owners of the Overgate Centre, for all their assistance.

Finally, we owe our appreciation to the many people who volunteered their memories of living and working in the Overgate and without whose reminiscences this book would have been greatly under-nourished.